Never More Than You Can Handle

Never More Than You Can Handle

JASON STIERWALT

StoryTerrace

CONTENTS

PROLOGUE: SMASHED

I should not be here.

The semi truck carrying a 125-foot base of a wind turbine, which had been traveling north, crossed the center line and crashed into me on August 17, 2011. I was driving south on Highway 108 in Oklahoma, near Glencoe, heading to work in Stillwater. The hitch pin on the semi's back axel, which was supposed to anchor the turn, had slipped out. Jackknifing, the semi sideswiped the whole south lane. My lane. I steered to avoid impact, driving into a ditch. But I still got hit. Sheering off the top, the crash crumpled my truck and crushed the sides. Severely injured and bleeding, I was in bad shape. EMTs said I was fighting them as they pulled me out of a two-by-two cubby square on the floorboard and strapped me onto a gurney. My lungs had collapsed, punctured on impact. My ankle shattered. My head gaped with a quarter-sized hole, impaled with the gear shift.

After ambulance drivers rushed me to the emergency room, a helicopter life flighted me to the St. Francis Medical Center in Tulsa.

Sticking by my side day and night in the hospital, my mom agonized that she'd lose me, my injuries were so bad. I have no memories of the crash. I was thirty-five years old, lying in a coma in a hospital bed, fighting for my life.

DODG

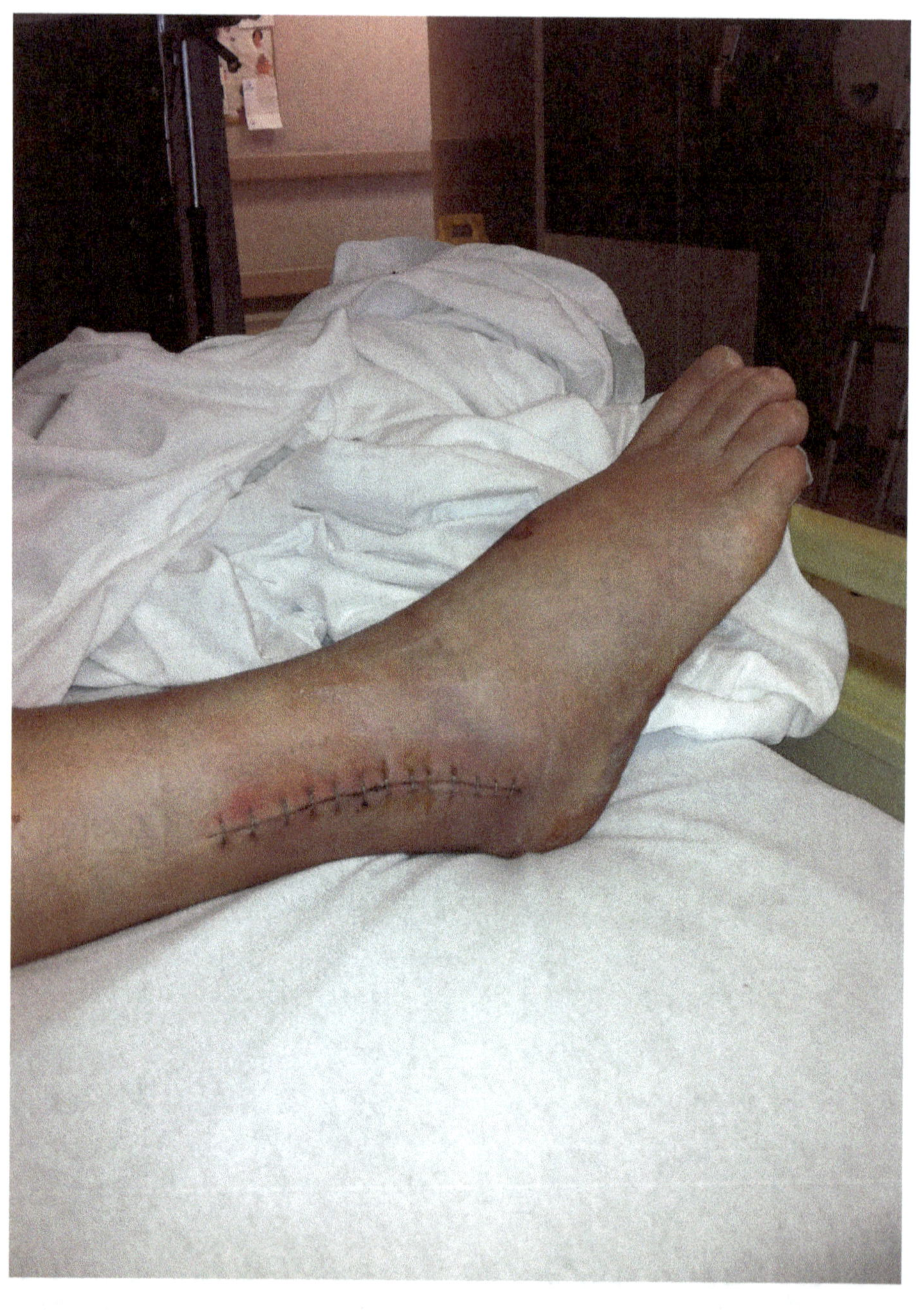

23/12

55%
5:10
Sat, April 13
OKLAHOMA
OU
OU
To start Bixby, press and hold the Bixby key.

1. RAISED RIGHT

It's better to tell the fricken' truth, no matter what. My mom and her sister Cindy both got pregnant at the same time. My mom was eighteen, and my aunt Cindy was seventeen. Grandpa got mad, sending them away to live in a home for unwed mothers, which was like an outreach house, until they gave birth. That's where mom lived when I was born in Oklahoma City on December 10, 1975. There is a story about the man who fathered me, but I didn't want to break my mom to find out what happened. If he didn't put in effort to come find me, then I wouldn't make the effort either. He wasn't part of my life, and I didn't know about him until I was eighteen.

Mom met another man, Mike Stierwalt, and married him. When I was two years old, he adopted me. I consider him my dad. I loved him. He is one hundred percent my dad, who raised me. I never saw my parents fight. They raised me right, making sure I respected adults and teachers, and disciplining me when I screwed up. I followed the Golden Rule and obeyed my parents. If I wanted to be treated well, I had to treat others well. All my life, I held the door open for people, and I checked in on them to see if they were okay. When I visited my relatives like my granny, my mom's mom, or my grandma Stierwalt, I gave them a hug. My parents made me mind. Every couple of months, we attended church. I wasn't much of a churchgoer when I was a kid.

My mom, Arnetta, she's a hardworking and humble woman. She didn't try to make a big name for herself. She was always there for me, supporting me when I was little and at sports events when I was in high school. When I'd wear out my jeans from hauling hay, she'd fix the holes in them. Cooking and cleaning, she was the housewife, staying home with the kids. My brother, Shane, is three and a half years younger than me, and my baby sister, Amando Jo, is twelve years younger than me. She's always been the more religious one, saying grace at big family dinners and praying. I like to say my sister didn't talk much when she was little, like one, two or three. But man, when she did start talking, there wasn't anything that could shut her up! I love my little sister. Shane and me, we were always getting into it. We played hard.

Mom always expected us to brush our teeth twice a day, and she made us eat what was on our plates, even if we didn't like it.

"You will sit there until you try it or go hungry until morning."

I remember one time when she served cream of corn, I knew it was going to be bad.

"You have got to try it," Mom said. I knew I wouldn't like it. She made me eat it. It was gross. I threw up a bunch of times.

She finally said, "You don't have to eat it anymore. You can get up from the table."

I did get spankings when I was growing up. At first, when I was little, like from ages one to five, it was my mom. She'd use the flyswatter or switch on me. When I got to be five or six, when the switch or swatter wasn't working anymore, she'd say, "Wait until your dad gets home."

Waiting was hell on a kid, I worried for a few hours, getting all nervous. Because when he came home, I got the belt. It's all part of discipline, and I understand that now. But then, I got worn out, waiting and worrying. My dad disciplined me well with that belt. As a kid, I got disciplined, especially if I was fighting with my brother. We were always roughhousing and getting into trouble. We'd play baseball and football, running in the yard. Playing football, Shane ended up breaking his collarbone. A month later, he broke the other one. Dad bought me and my brother boxing gloves. Anytime we had an argument, we'd get out those boxing gloves. Because I was so much taller, I'd have to get down on my knees, boxing him.

Dad was always fair, teaching me to respect people. He also showed how to work hard, laboring in the oil fields. At one point in his twenties, he lost his job. The company gave him the option to go to Hobbs, New Mexico, or get a payout and get laid off. He got laid off. We didn't have a lot of money, it was hard being poor. My mom didn't really work until I was a teenager, she was always taking care of us kids. With no heat or air conditioning in our house, I felt miserable in the hot summers. My room was on the second floor. To cool off, I took a cold shower or propped up a fan in front of the window before I could fall asleep. When I was in elementary school, Dad got a job selling chemicals for the oil field and later moved up into management. He's worked at the same company for forty-five years. When I was growing up, he also teamed up with his brother, my uncle Mark, working for ranchers. He was always the financial guy, and my uncle did the hard labor.

As a kid, we moved around to a couple of places. I know I was five when I started kindergarten, I was living in Foraker, Oklahoma. It was a great place to grow up. I attended school in the area from kindergarten until I graduated high school and moved out of the house. Foraker itself didn't have a school. We were bussed to Shidler, a town nearby. A person who drove a station wagon, which served as our bus, picked up the kids. The average number of kids on the bus was six. While some kids started to ride at 6 am, I climbed on the bus at 7 am. I was glad I didn't have to get up as early as those other kids. I had twenty-three people in my graduating class, and only four of those were girls.

My dentist used to joke, "That's about all there is to Foraker, it's about four acres."

While I lived there, Foraker had about thirty to forty people. There were ten to eleven houses in the whole town, with a few old buildings. My block had four houses in it. There was a church down the road from us, but not many stores. Because there was not a lot to do, we had our own fun picking asparagus or playing in the creek. We'd ride bikes, miles and miles a day, wearing out our tires. Grabbing our fishing poles, we'd pedal out to the creek, do some fishing, then ride home. Sometimes with a couple of friends, we rode our bikes downtown, past the building that said, "Grocery Store." It's not operating there anymore. Because we didn't have a grocery store in Foraker, we drove about an hour to

Pawhuska to buy food, which had to last a long time, about four weeks. We made do until we took another trip to town. Towards the end of the month, when food was running out, I remember we ate a lot of hot dogs and baloney sandwiches, trying to get by.

What amazed me is we never had to lock our vehicles. We left our keys in the car. If someone needed a vehicle moved, he could get right in the truck and move it out of the way. Foraker used to be a great big city, a boom town, forged from oil in the ground and ranching. Back then, the oil flowed, and people made a lot of money from the oil. A railroad ran through town, transporting oil from the refineries and goods into town. I remember seeing pictures of Foraker, with lots of buildings and people. It seemed like it had thousands of people. When the railroad shut down, the town shut down, too. It's a small community now, considered a ghost town. There is a YouTube video about Foraker being a ghost town, with all the empty buildings run down and people gone. Even with all the people who have left, I still consider Foraker my home. I'm a firm believer that Osage County, where Foraker is located, is God's country, with cattle ranches, prairie grass, and oil rigs stretching across the land.

2. FAMILY GATHERINGS

All through childhood, I visited my relatives, enjoying family gatherings. My mom took me out to visit my granny, her mom, who lived in the country. We drove there almost every weekend. She lived about an hour away. Her husband, my grandpa, was a World War II Vet. When he was younger, he was always good at working on machinery, like back hoes and skid loaders. He stayed pretty busy his whole life, working maintenance on a ranch over by Bartlesville. While he fixed the equipment, Granny was at home, raising my first cousin, Steven. My aunt Cindy, the one who was pregnant at the same time as my mom, had a boy, Steven. He loved his mom, but she was not the one who raised him. My granny did.

He was my best friend growing up. We always messed around. Back then, you were always outside. As soon as you woke up, you ate breakfast, raced outside, and didn't come home until the streetlights came on. We hunted and fished in the creek, which ran through their property. Together as toddlers and through elementary school, we played the whole day outdoors on weekends when I visited. Even in winter, we'd romp in the snow until we couldn't feel our hands. When I was five or six, my granny sewed clothes for us, me and my cousin, to help us out, being so poor. She was a good woman. She'd make us corduroy pants and pearl snap shirts. I was embarrassed wearing those corduroys to school. The sound of scritch, scritch as you walked in them was annoying. It just wasn't the right style. All the other kids at school had jeans. When I look back, those pearl snap shirts weren't very popular then, and I didn't like them. Nowadays, those pearl snap shirts are more popular. When Steven moved away in third grade, I missed playing with him at Granny's place.

I saw my other grandma, Grandma Stierwalt, my dad's mom, every three or four weeks. She was the greatest woman. A godly woman, she knew the Bible and always said grace before every meal. Never speaking ill of people, she acknowledged that she didn't like a certain behavior, then moseyed on. Her actions of how she loved her relationship with Jesus are something I vividly remember. She spent her days actively walking and talking with Jesus. When she got up in the morning, she prayed and did a morning devotional. At lunchtime, she prayed. After reading her Bible in the afternoons, she studied her verse cards. Before she went to bed, she meditated again. I can remember hearing her humming hymns while washing the dishes at the kitchen sink that faced east. She'd look out the window, soaking up the view. Her house was a place of solitude. I can remember going to stay with her one time to study because it was a peaceful, quiet place.

She was a tiny woman, maybe four foot eleven. She had a big heart. Because Grandpa had died at an early age, she had lived by herself for fifty years. I was only four or five when he had a heart attack and passed away. She grew up poor. When she was young, her family used a stove that you had to put wood into. They baked biscuits and gravy. The stove heated up the house, especially in the hot and sticky summer. As a little girl, she liked cooking and baking and still enjoyed it as she became an adult. When I visited her as a kid, she was always feeding us.

"Are you hungry?"

"No, Grandma."

"Do you need something?"

"No, Grandma, I'm fine."

She'd make us eat something even if we were not hungry. She'd serve homemade biscuits and gravy at lunch. In the evening, it would be peanut butter and jelly. Sometimes, she changed it up, giving me a pimento cheese sandwich.

"What's this?"

"Just try it," she said.

When I drove with her, I always worried. She drove a boat, one of those big Ford LTDs. She was so little she could barely see over the steering wheel. From my viewpoint, sitting in the back, it was like she was looking at the sky. My sister and I used to joke about getting taller than her. "I'm nine, and look, I'm almost as tall as Grandma!" When we got to be twelve, we all were taller than her.

Most weekends, she took me to church, the same Nazarene church she attended for fifty years. I knew she had Blackjack Gum in her purse, it tasted like black licorice. It was nasty, but I still liked it. I'd be sitting there in the pew, in the middle of the service, asking, "Grandma, do you have any gum?" She always gave me a piece.

She passed on goodness to the next generation. I see how well she treated her kids, my dad, my uncle Mark, and his two sisters, my Aunt Cheryl and Aunt Kay. She had a big impact on my life. My relatives on the Stierwalt side always welcomed me.

I miss those Sunday dinners, it was like a seven-course meal. My Aunt Cheryl lived up on the hill, and her husband was a big gardener. He grew the best vegetables. We had fresh green beans, fried okra, and corn on the cob. We'd eat two or three different kinds of meats, like roast beef, chicken, or turkey. In the end, Aunt Cheryl served a whole plate of sweets, sometimes five different kinds. We had brownies, cherry cheesecake, and sugar cookies. When we got together, that's what my mom brought. She made good sugar cookies. While the adults were talking inside, I'd hang out with cousins who were my age. We sat outside on the porch, swinging on the swing and talking away the day. My cousins and I played basketball or fished. Grabbing a couple of poles, we'd go pond hopping. I remember with one cousin, we built forts, with tunnels and dens, in the barn in the haymow. Usually, my cousins had some sort of animal, chickens or horses. When I was a teenager, we'd go hunting or saddle the horses to go riding. Growing up, we had no covers while hunting deer. We jumped out of a truck or sprang out of a ditch. These days in Pawnee, the hunters sit on a deer stand, waiting for the prey to come. It's just not the same.

I miss those days, getting together with our families. I remember that we used to have family reunions on both sides. Aunts and uncles, cousins, we all knew each other, gathering a couple of times a year at Christmas, Thanksgiving, and birthdays. It's sad now that we don't get together as families.

My girls just don't know their cousins like I did when I was growing up. It might be four weeks after Christmas until we can figure out a time when all of us can meet. As a kid, my granny and Grandma Stierwalt and my aunties and uncles always made those occasions special.

Their encouragement and faith, along with my dad and Uncle Mark's insistence on working and doing chores, helped me get along in life.

3. CHORES

My family instilled the importance of gathering, and expected me to do chores. When I was young, about seven or eight, I pushed the lawn mower to the electric company down the street. After mowing, I pushed the lawn mower back to the house. I made ten dollars. The next summer, I was mowing more lawns, two or three of them.

Starting when I was nine, I fed the horses, and the dogs. My dad was a horse trader. At one end of town, my dad leased land where the horses were kept. After buying horses, he rode and broke them for thirty to sixty days, later selling them for profit. I never knew how many horses I'd be feeding, it varied from about three to eight. Most days, I could shake the bucket of feed and the horses trotted over to eat. I remember one time, one of those horses was stubborn, staying in the field. Using the lead rope and halter, I pulled on him. He wouldn't come.

I ran to talk to dad, who was in the barn. "Dad, I can't catch the horses!"

"Hold on. I will be right there."

Before he came to help me, I decided to do it myself. I jumped on one horse, riding bareback and kicking its side. That old horse spooked. He stopped suddenly, sticking his hooves in the dirt. I flew over his head and landed in the dust, stunned. I lay there shaken for a few minutes, but wasn't hurt too bad. I picked myself up and kept going. I'm stubborn, and hardheaded, just like that horse.

At the other end of town, my dad raised greyhounds to chase and hunt coyotes. I rode my bike there after school to feed them. If you've never seen a greyhound catching a coyote, you're missing out. Those dogs were expensive. I'm not sure how he afforded those dogs, he had ten of them. I knew how much it cost to feed those dogs, I don't think my mom ever knew. I was amazed how much they ate, being so skinny. They consumed a 50-lb sack every couple of days, which cost ten to fifteen dollars each. That was three hundred dollars a month back in the nineties.

Come hunting day, Dad had me pack those greyhounds in his truck, five on each side in boxes.

"Make sure you place the dogs in the right boxes."

On the mornings we went coyote hunting, he named the dogs he wanted loaded and what side to put them on. Some dogs worked better together than others. The dogs that were one hundred percent greyhound were let loose to catch the coyotes, and some dogs which were part Irish/Wolfhound followed after to kill the coyote.

I would get in trouble if I mixed them up. Dad and his buddies revved their trucks, sometimes seventy five miles per hour, careening through the field. When someone spotted a coyote, they yelled and released the dogs. I understand the thrill of it all, it is addicting, seeing them greyhound haul butt after those coyotes, and catching them. I understand the need to have a hobby. Shoot, everyone needs to have a hobby, otherwise you'd go crazy. But dang, it was dangerous sometimes. Not seeing a cliff, my dad drove over it and wrecked the whole front end of his truck.

Besides helping with the dogs, I also hauled more hay bales than anyone I know. My uncle Mark and my dad hired me to work for them. Dad was the financial guy behind the operation, and my uncle did the hard work. By the time I was thirteen, they had me driving a one-ton truck with no power steering. It took all I had in my britches to turn that wheel. I couldn't see very well to stay straight in the field. The crew stacked the bales on the truck and then painstakingly unloaded them in the barn. When I was a little older, I helped on the back of the truck.

Starting from when we got out of school in May through September, we hauled a lot of hay, sometimes more than 100,000 square bales in a season. When I was about sixteen, Dad and my uncle purchased a Hay Monster, which made hauling more efficient. The machine, which has a spout that spews out the hay, makes hay rounds instead of squares. I made enough in one year, $1500, to buy my first vehicle. I remember I saw it on Truck Trader, it was a 1969 Chevy Stepaside. After me and Dad drove to Blackwell, about an hour away, to pick it up, we discovered the truck was a stick shift. The gears were "three on the tree."

"I didn't know how to drive this thing!" I was sixteen years old and didn't have a clue how to drive it.

On the hour-long trip home, with the gears grinding a lot, I figured out how to drive it. I never liked asking for help. If I couldn't figure something out, I tried my darndest to get it on my own.

Lugging 2,000 to 3,000 bales a day, I muscled up, being in the best shape of my life. I didn't have much body fat. I credit my uncle for teaching me to work hard. Not requiring much, my uncle just expected me to show up. If you show up every day and try, you will make it.

4. SPORTS AND SCHOOL

Showing up was how I made it through school. Rising early and riding the station wagon bus from Foraker to Shidler, I got there and did my work, getting mostly As and Bs. I didn't have to study a lot. Some friends, five or six of us, I knew from kindergarten through high school. We were still hanging out as I got older. We were close. When I was in school, I was the quiet one, not wanting to speak up. My classmates voted me "Most Shy."

As a kid, I practiced basketball every night, trying to perfect my shot. By the time I got to high school, I was pretty good at a lot of sports. My parents always showed up for me, making it to all my ball games, like sports events at Shidler High School. They attended every game, even when I played summer ball, supporting me.

My dad was always saying, "You should have done such and such, and you would have done better in the game."

I appreciated it when they came to my games. They were glad about me being in sports. I played quarterback in football, basketball, and baseball. I loved playing athletics. My parents paid gas money so I could get to games and practices, but wouldn't pay much more than that. Once when I wanted a new pair of basketball shoes, I asked if I could get them.

"The shoes cost one hundred dollars."

"We can't afford that! You will have to pay half the cost," my mom said. Reluctantly, they bucked up half, which was fifty dollars.

We were such a small school that we played eight-man football instead of the traditional eleven-man team. Our team had about fifteen to eighteen players instead of the fifty to sixty that a lot of bigger schools had. If you showed up for practice, you made the team. We didn't throw the ball, it was mostly a running game. The sports seasons always overlapped. As you played the last football game, you were already practicing basketball. When you nearly finished basketball, you were out cracking the bat for baseball.

Most memories of playing ball were good, but some were bad. I always pressed through, persevering. I was stubborn that way, not letting pain get me down. When I was a sophomore, me and this kid Chris Brown were jumping on a trampoline at a friend's house right before a basketball game. He jumped before me, launching me into the air. My arm crashed through a window in a garage nearby. It didn't even hurt. When I pulled my arm out, the glass had cut a big chunk of my arm. I tore off the skin and threw it on the ground. If I had saved it, doctors could have put stitches in it. Not thinking much of the cuts and blood, I wrapped it with an ace bandage and drove to the school with my buddies. As I hopped on the bus for basketball, my coach saw the bandages.

"What happened to your arm?"

"Oh, I don't know. I cut it somehow. It's no big deal."

"Let me see." I unwrapped my arm.

"You are going to the hospital." He benched me for that game. When nurses began to clean the area, it really started to hurt. Holy cow, I almost came unglued then. I could see my bone sticking out as they were preparing the area for the skin graft. It hurt like hell. Always tough, I pushed through. I wanted to play ball again.

During my junior year, we were scrimmaging on the field one week before the first football game. As I threw the ball, two guys picked me up and slammed me to the ground. I broke my collarbone.

Wanting me to get back to playing as soon as possible, Dad took me to a lot of doctors.

"When can my son play ball again?"

He kept asking until he got the right answer. The first doctor said I'd be out the entire season. The second doctor said seven weeks. The third doctor said in four weeks, I could play again. We took his word. That was rough, not playing. I missed four games. We were really good that year. Even while I was out recovering, the team was winning all their games.

I have enormous respect for my football coach in high school, Matt Holland, who did things right.

He drilled into us, "There is no "I" in team," expecting 110 percent. He made me a better player and person, expecting so much.

Whether we lost or won, we always watched the films on Sunday or Monday, trying to improve. He showed us where we messed up, and we'd practice. We lifted weights, this was in the nineties, long before lifting was popular. Practicing, especially the two-a-days before school started, was tough. After hauling hay through the night until 4 am, we'd sleep for a few hours, then get up, ready to head out to the football field by 6 am. By 8 a.m., we swam in the pool. After hauling more hay in the afternoon, we practiced football again in full pads, sweat dripping in the 100-degree heat. I was in the best shape of my life, burning a lot of calories. I remember eating four of five baloney sandwiches and drinking a lot of Natural Light beer to get through hauling hay and practices. Weighing 170 pounds in high school, I had zero percent body fat. All the hard work paid off. In my senior year, four of us made the All-State team, and we won most of our games.

5. PARTYING

I was a heathen as a teenager, pretty rambunctious. I shot a lot of deer illegally and drank a lot. We partied, always finding those spots; we had three or four of them where we hung out. Our football coach knew we liked to drink beer on Friday and Saturday nights. If we missed a practice or if we were late, we had to run laps or lift more weights. The cops knew but somehow didn't stop us. They said, "Don't be driving around. And don't get caught."

When I was nineteen, I got caught. Hanging with a bunch of Shidler people, we partied on the way down to a float trip on the river. We drank beer, getting drunk on the way. When one guy wanted cigarettes, I agreed to buy them for him. I had a fake ID. I shouldn't have been driving. I lost control of the truck, hitting a fence post. One passenger got ejected, smacking the barbed wire. When the State Patrol administered a sobriety test, I failed it.

I spent the night in jail. The next day, I saw the judge. When the guy in front of me, who was in for his second DUI, only got more probation, I figured the judge would be lenient with me.

Instead, the judge lit into me, yelling. "You are in trouble. What were you thinking, driving drunk? I don't want to see you here again. I'm fining you $7,000 for using a fake ID and DUI. If you keep your record clean, all the charges will be taken off."

I didn't abide by the rules. I've been to jail three times, all alcohol-related.

6. LOVE OF MY LIFE

All through high school, I dated the same girl. She was one year behind me in school. My parents didn't approve of our relationship.

"You shouldn't be with her. She's too young."

I was young and dumb, not listening to what they said. When I was eighteen, we got pregnant. When my daughter Brittnee was born, she was the love of my life. That girl meant everything to me.

After graduating high school, I headed to Northeastern Oklahoma University in the fall of 1994, where I had a chance to play baseball. My parents helped pay the cost. Inspired by my high school football coach, Matt Holland, I figured I'd get a degree and coach like him. I was living in the dorms and attending classes with the baseball players. I hated living in the dorms. Those guys acted like asses, they were buttheads, always mouthing off and arrogant. College wasn't for me. I lasted only about a month. I felt bad that my parents had spent all that money, and it was wasted when I quit. I knew I wasn't providing very well for my daughter and thought, "*Man, I need to get a job.*" I quit school, trying to figure out a better way.

In Oklahoma, you have only a few choices. You either work on a ranch or in the refineries. Only one or two of the twenty-three people I graduated with decided to attend college. I got a great job when I was nineteen, working on the road and traveling with the oil refineries. I was making great money, per diem, going from Boston to Florida to Texas. Though I enjoyed traveling, I always liked coming home to Oklahoma again. Sometimes people in other cities were rude. Where I live in Oklahoma, the people are a lot more friendly. For a time, me and my girlfriend and Brittnee all lived together, seeing each other every day. I enjoyed watching my daughter grow up. About a year into it, my girlfriend started doing some crazy stuff that I didn't approve of. We ended up splitting up.

When she got custody of Brittnee, that messed my whole world up. When we broke up, I was devastated. I went from seeing her every day to every other weekend. Her mom moved around a lot. In order to see my daughter, I might have to travel up to three hours away to pick her up. It was not the nicest breakup. We were never married, but our breakup felt like a divorce. I still had to pay child support. It messed me up not seeing Brittnee.

7. SINGLE AND STRIVING FOR BETTER

I started rebuilding my life after Brittnee and my ex-girlfriend left, working in the oil fields. When they offered me a crappy job, I knew I didn't want to do that for all my life.

When I was twenty-four, I jumped back into college at Tonkawa, taking online classes with all the younger students. Maybe because I was older, I paid attention, trying to better myself. I studied, striving for an associate degree in mechanical engineering. That time around, because I was on my own and didn't have to rely on my parent's income, I got a lot of grants to pay for tuition and books. One semester, I received one thousand dollars extra to help out with costs. It was really nice. Unlike a lot of students who didn't come to class and flunked out, I showed up. I did well in college, getting As and B's. While working at a machine shop forty hours a week, trying to pay rent and child support, and going to school in the evenings, I was busting ass, but I made it.

I cycled through a few jobs, then landed at Armstrong Flooring, where I worked for sixteen years. I loved that job. We teamed together, you'd see your crew members more than your family. When something broke, you all worked to fix it. You trusted your coworkers. You could leave your wallet out, not worrying about someone taking it. When reviews came up, all the workers scored each employee and had to approve for bonuses.

While juggling school and work, I pushed into Taekwondo, striving to get in shape. Taekwondo tenets promote courtesy, self-control, an indomitable spirit, perseverance, and respect. I hold all of those words close to me. Rising through the ranks, I earned my black belt and was halfway to my second black belt in five years, by going at least two times a week for all that time. We were expected to show courtesy and respect.

When we entered the room, we bowed to the master or anyone who taught us. If a five-year-old with a black belt came in or someone with a higher rank, we bowed to him. If someone took time to teach us, we listened and told them thank you. Seeing the American flag, we bowed. We bowed as we entered to practice on the mat called a dojo.

When you attended camps, you kept pushing yourself. I've been pushed in my life where I felt physically worn out, like in football practice with Coach Holland or hauling hay. But while attending those camps for Taekwondo when I was in my twenties, I knew my body could do more.

My instructors always said, "You can trick your mind to do more than you think."

If you were tired, you told your mind, "*Do more, you've got more in you.*"

You had to be on guard, ready to defend yourself. While training, you set goals, striving to attain that higher belt. With fewer belts, it didn't take much time. But between the red and black belts, you spent months training. For me, it was a year to a year and a half before I was ready to test for the black belt.

They'd throw you in a ring, where you'd put on your gear and sparred with two other people who had achieved four or five black belts. All they did, whatever you threw at them, they'd block, block, block. Wearing headgear, you fought to protect yourself.

I thought, "*These guys are good.*" Even though they held higher belts, they still took time to teach us.

I still respect the voices of the masters. "You must preserve," they said. "Continue to struggle against all odds, and you will succeed. You cannot give up. There are too many people watching you to quit. Push through and persevere."

Struggling against all odds, perservering, and overcoming have become an important part of my life. I know I can't quit when things get hard. When something is coming at you, you block it. At first, I didn't know how to do a roundhouse kick. But after doing it five thousand times over five years, I practiced and figured it out. That roundhouse kick is ingrained in my brain. I never went there to fight others. The classes I took were more about self-defense. Taking Taekwondo, I became more confident. You have to do it right, with excellence.

Etiquette is a big deal in Taekwondo, you can't do things half-assed. I've always been a hard worker, but Taekwondo ramped that up for me. I can't see stuff lying around and not fix it. I will go out of my way to do it. There are situations when time is of the essence, and you have to hurry to finish. Not liking to go back and fix it again, I did it right the first time. I don't like lazy people or whiners or when they lie to cover up their laziness. Instead of listening to people whine, I did the job myself. Taekwondo instilled the indomitable spirit of having the courage to stand up for your beliefs. When bad days come, you need self-control. If you have a bunch of stuff happening, self-control helps you think positively. I don't get outraged or stay mad for very long. If someone is talking down to me, I try to bring them up.

The Bible talks about that. Sometimes you will have bad days, and it's how you persevere that matters to God. I'm a firm believer that God won't give you more than you can handle, even if it means dealing with someone who became addicted to drugs.

8. DESTRUCTION OF DRUGS

I was twenty-five when I met Amanda, I enjoyed her enthusiasm. She was bubbly and fun. She's the opposite of me, always speaking her mind. She's not afraid to hurt your feelings. I'm the total opposite. If it hurts you, I don't say it.

My roommate was dating her twin sister and introduced me to her. She was pretty, five years younger than me. She was going to school, learning to cut hair at Po Tech. We dated for a year before we moved in together. I should have paid attention in the beginning. As soon as we moved in, we started fighting. I never saw my parents fighting, but Amanda's parents argued when I was around. That's how Amanda and I were, always tearing into each other.

Even with all the fighting, we eventually married. We had two daughters together, Delaney and Hadleigh, who are everything to me. I would take a bullet for them. I worked full-time at Armstrong Flooring in the maintenance department, providing for our family. The weekends were tense. My wife treated Brittnee, my oldest daughter, like hell, always being mean. She put a dagger into our relationship, driving a wedge between us. Amanda didn't like Brittnee and she didn't like Brittnee's mom. She didn't like that I had to pay child support. Not wanting to fight with her, I agreed to what she said most of the time. When I had to stop seeing Brittnee every other weekend, I felt crushed.

Amanda started running around partying and doing drugs. When she was gone, I'd be taking care of the girls. When she was home, we argued. I stuck through a lot, trying to hold our family together. I remembered how hard it was not seeing Brittnee after my first breakup for all those years. I didn't want to go through that again.

I wish my daughters could remember how Amanda was in the good days when I first married her.

Drugs destroyed my marriage and my family. Meth is bad in these small towns. I'm one hundred percent honest. It's better to tell the fricken' truth, even if it's something people don't want to hear. Everything I tell you is one hundred percent honest. When my wife started using drugs, she became angry, yelling and screaming. She'd leave the house, being gone most of the night. Meth hits hard. You can tell by their teeth, and how skinny they get. Her eyeballs sunk into her head. My wife was as skinny as a rail, thinking everyone was after her. If someone drove by, she'd get all panicky.

"They're coming to get me!"

When she started talking crazy like that, I didn't know what to do with her.

People on drugs don't care about anyone, just themselves and getting the next high. Always cranky, she stopped caring about the family and our relationship deteriorated.

She started stealing stuff, to get more drugs. If she worked, she used the money to pay off debts or buy more drugs. She was always getting high, and made my life hell. Unable to keep fighting for our marriage, I wanted out.

9. NO MEMORIES

Because of my wife's drug addiction and all the crazy going on, I needed out and filed for divorce. At that time, I was not living in the house in Pawnee with my wife. I was staying at a house that we had owned when we lived in Ralston, where her twin sister lived. I remember going to court around nine in the morning on August 17, 2011, but nothing much was solved that day. The whole thing took only fifteen minutes, and the proceedings were postponed.

At ten-thirty that morning, I drove my Dodge pickup truck, heading south on Highway 108 towards my job in Stillwater. Just outside of Glencoe, a semi-truck barreled in my direction. That is all I remember about the crash that nearly killed me. Eyewitnesses, the Oklahoma State Patrol, and EMTs all filed reports, filling in details.

An Anderson semi-truck carrying a 125-foot base of a wind turbine was traveling north on 108. A driver of a smaller company truck from Anderson followed behind, monitoring progress. She noticed that something had broken off from the back of the semi. The hitch pin, designed to anchor the truck's back axles, had slipped out. Before she could notify the front driver, the semi crossed the center line, sideswiping all the lanes and cutting into traffic. OHP reports showed that I tried to avoid impact by steering off into the ditch by a barbed wire fence. The truck still rammed me. Sheering off the cab, the crash smashed my doors and crushed the top.

Shoved to the floorboard, I was pinned inside, trapped in a two-foot by two-foot cubby under the steering wheel. As the paramedics attempted to rescue me, they said I fought them.

"You were in fight or flight, flinging your arms and resisting. It took three or four of us to hold you down."

When they strapped me onto the gurney, I was in bad shape, injured, and bleeding all over. My lungs were punctured, which made it hard to breathe. My ankle shattered, bones fragmented, barely hanging on. My head gaped with a wound the size of a quarter, impaled with what I think must have been the gear shift.

The ambulance rushed me to the hospital in Tulsa, then life-flighted me to St. Francis Medical Center in Tulsa. Sticking by my side, my mom worried she'd lose me. She stayed with me day and night, agonizing. I have no memories of the crash or laying in a coma near death for nearly two weeks.

10. ON THE EDGE

As I sprawled there unconscious, Mom fretted. The heart monitor beeped, and a ventilator hummed, breathing life, taking the job of my punctured lungs. Hooked to the pole near the bed, IVs dripped fluids into my veins. Doctors kept me in a coma, my injuries were so bad. The gaping hole in my head was bandaged. Fearing that I suffered a traumatic brain injury, doctors carefully monitored the swelling in my brain. Surgeons reconnected my busted ankle bones, inserting a five-inch screw and metal plates. I never knew, never remember my time at St. Francis. While struggling to survive, I was unaware of life around me.

People who visited me said, "We were having conversations that only me and you knew about. Do you remember that?" I don't remember them coming to see me.

The Stillwater News, which reported on the crash the next day, said OHP had smelled alcohol on my breath and the whole accident was under investigation.

My mom was aware, alert and tense, watching me struggle. Through the agonizing days and nights, mom stuck with me, staying by my side and praying. She suffered sleepless nights and restless days, with the constant flow of medical professionals entering my room to check on my progress.

"When the nurses came in to check your vitals, they turned on the lights. All hours of the day and through the night, they'd come in. I was exhausted. I thought I'd lose you, that you wouldn't make it through."

For days, my prognosis didn't look good. All banged up, I wasn't given much chance to survive. To help her cope and get support, Mom started a Facebook group. More than one hundred people joined the group, praying for me and sending encouraging notes, lifting me up to the Lord. I can imagine my Grandma Stierwalt, who had passed away in 1995, was probably praying, too. When I was a kid visiting her, she prayed all through the day, walking and talking with Jesus.

11. ANSWERED PRAYERS

Somewhere in that two-week period, when I was in a coma, I began to turn around, showing signs of life. Somehow, I started coming back. As my lungs started working on their own, doctors took me off life support. When I responded, Mom was surprised and relieved.

"You've come back!"

But that was only the beginning. I faced months of intense rehab as doctors and therapists helped to mend my broken body. They were worried about my head injury. I saw four or five different doctors, including neurologists, psychologists, and surgeons, and even a top-notch neurologist in Florida. They kept doing all these brain scans and cognitive tests, like what you would use for kids. Initially, my head throbbed from the pain. I took pain meds and also a blood thinner because of a blood clot.

My memory returned after about two weeks. I remember riding in the ambulance to the Jim Thorpe Rehab Center in Tulsa, jacking with the paramedics on the way. I hate hospitals, and I didn't want to be there. My goal was to leave and get out. Fighting, I kept trying to climb out of the bed.

The medical staff told me, "You kept trying to leave. We had to strap you to the bed so you wouldn't go outside."

When people visited, they would say, "You were talking sweet to me, trying to get me to unstrap you."

It was rough lying there. I was used to getting up, working hard, pushing through. At the time, I had been lifting weights at the gym and in good shape. In some ways, all that working out helped me. All that Taekwondo training kicked in, of persevering and overcoming, as I pushed through therapy. I remember the nurses at Jim Thorpe were really nice to me. Doing a lot of mobility stuff, and the staff pushed me. They lifted me out of my seat to see if I could stand. The doctor didn't want me to put weight on that ankle. Wrecked from nerve damage, it hurt all the time, like it burned. Even though the surgeon used two metal plates and inserted screws at different angles to repair my bones, my ankle never worked right again.

When I got out of rehab, I returned to Pawnee, where I had lived with my wife. Our divorce had been postponed because of the accident. For her, all she could think about was the payout that I might get from the accident. She was still on drugs, doing her crazy stuff. After cutting hair there at the house, she would leave about nine at night and be gone the whole time. I wondered where she was going. I was in a wheelchair, trying to take care of my girls. I didn't like being in a wheelchair. I'm the worst about asking for help. Stubborn, I would rather do it all myself, and got good at maneuvering after two or three days. Going crazy from boredom at home, I just wanted to get back to work, where I scheduled maintenance for the flooring company. There are only so many crossword puzzles that I could do and TV shows I could watch. I missed about a month and a half, maybe two months at the most. Once I finished using the wheelchair, they put me in a walking boot.

Even when I finally returned to work, I still needed more rehab. My mom shuttled me back and forth to Stillwater. Those therapists scared me when they moved my ankle, sometimes three or four inches in each session. Taking it under their arm, they torqued my joints. I cried out, it hurt so bad. But turns out I needed that much therapy. They taught me how to walk again, putting heel to toe and practicing.

When I was at Armstrong, I worked 12-hour shifts for two weeks, then rotated to day shifts. I couldn't sleep during the day, only about three or four hours. After the accident, I struggled and was not sleeping well. I was getting mad at everyone, like road rage. The doctor gave me antidepressants and Trazodone, which helped me sleep better.

I had so many doctor's appointments with the brain doctor, my regular doctor, and my ankle doctor. I thought my brain was slipping when I couldn't remember all the appointments. When the appointments slowed down, my memory started recovering, getting way, way better. Doctors were surprised. Except for a few headaches, I don't have much trouble with my head.

But even with all the rehab, I still can't run with that ankle. Months after it happened, I wished they'd cut my friggen foot off, there was so much nerve damage. It was stinging. Even now, my foot swells when I use it too much.

During this rehab process, a couple of significant things happened. I had a girl come to my door, whom I didn't know, saying that my wife and her husband were together. It totally blindsided me. When I confronted my wife about it, she totally denied being with that guy but did admit to doing meth with him. Frustrated with my wife and crazy behavior, I moved out to live with my parents. I love my parents, but being there as an adult just felt awkward. I rolled around in a wheelchair in their home, going crazy. During that time, authorities busted into my wife's house, and my wife was caught with drug paraphernalia in her home. I got temporary custody of the girls and picked them up. We eventually moved out to a house I was already in the process of buying before the accident. While dealing with all that, I was also involved in a lawsuit. My attorney filed a lawsuit, claiming negligence against the trucking company, whose semi truck crossed the median and hit my truck.

12. SETTLEMENT

My attorney Noble McIntyre headed the team, filing suit against the Anderson Trucking Service, the drivers of the semi-truck carrying the wind turbine and the maintenance truck following behind, and DMI Industries, the manufacturer and transporter of the wind turbine.

Initially, the Stillwater News Press had reported that OHP officers smelled alcohol on my breath at the crash scene and that alcohol might have been involved in the crash. I was aggravated about that accusation. I did have beer cans in the back of my truck, but I wouldn't have been drinking. I was on my way to work that day in Stillwater when the truck hit me. When the blood tests came out negative, I felt relieved. They also tested the semi-driver, and his results were negative.

Negotiating the lawsuit required a lot of communication between me and the attorney's office. The crash wrecked my body, and I suffered some long-term effects, especially with my ankle.

In an email, I described all the things wrong with me to McIntyre and Savannah, his legal assistant:

"Hey Savannah, I have been writing some things down when I can remember them that you or Noble might need. Things I suffer from.

-Back pain (mostly when I try to lie on my left side)

-I cannot sleep without some kind of sleep medicine. If I fall asleep without medicine, I will wake up like 2 hours later.

-It is painful to walk on my ankle. It would be better if I had pain medication, but I quit taking them.

-I cannot jog or run. Makes it hard to play with my girls.

-Constantly going to doctor appointments messes up my work schedule and numerous other things.

-Depression (no thoughts of killing myself or anything)

-The bottom of my foot and big toes are numb.

-Hard to put on my socks and jeans with the numbness.

-Can't really take a shower because I cannot stand on my right foot, I will lose my balance.

-I know I'm not as bright as I used to be. I always made A's and B's in High School and College.

-I always worry about if I lose my job if I would be able to get another job.

-My left kneecap is numb. Do not know if it's a nerve or what. I cannot walk on my knees.

-Lots of headaches. None really severe. A lot more than I used to have.

-I have people come up to me and say, "Man, you used to be huge what happened."

-I had been lifting for years. It will be hard to start back because I don't have much motivation and not much stamina.

-The scars I have, mostly the ones on my face, mess up my confidence. Being single is not good.

-My short-term memory is terrible. This is affecting my job.

I will send you more when get to it.

Thanks, Jason"

Besides indicating all the ways I was suffering, I also made a list of the doctor's appointments, which were extended for months. While McIntyre gathered evidence for my case, Anderson company officials visited my parents, trying to make things right.

"We're sorry this happened." They knew I would get a settlement, it meant a lot that they cared. It was not a long-drawn-out process.

Noble McIntyre worked hard for me, advocating for a large settlement, and we won the case. With the settlement money, I bought a pickup truck to replace the one that got wrecked, which I am still driving twelve years later, and 160 acres of land. I bought a house on five acres where I could live with my girls. A couple of years later, I also purchased a boat and a tractor. I did spend alot from that settlement, but the rest I invested with the second-largest financial firm in the nation. Even with the settlement, I am still working. I would go crazy if I didn't have anything to do.

13. MIRACLES

Looking back, I know God spared me for a reason; it was to take care of my girls. He knew that they would need me. If I had died in that wreck, I don't know what would have happened, with their mom on drugs and not able to watch them. When I recovered and no longer using the wheelchair, I drove to the junkyard, trying to salvage what I could from my wrecked truck. I really wanted my speakers and a few other things.

My friends said, "Jason, you won't salvage anything from that truck. It's all crumpled."

Determined and stubborn, I went anyway.

My heart sank when I saw my truck. It was sobering. The top was shaved off, and both sides were caved in. In the crash, that semi-truck pushed my truck down. In that moment, I knew that the crash really happened. I don't know how I survived that crash, I should have been crushed. The Lord was watching over me. Somehow, I saw that semi barreling toward me and dove into that little cubby on the floorboard below the bench seats. Huddling in that small space was what saved me.

I know the people who own the ranch where I steered my truck into the ditch, trying to avoid the wreck, and hit the barbed wire fence.

"When we saw your truck, we didn't know how you survived."

I started reading the posts on Facebook about how bad my crash was and how I was in a coma. My mom and all my friends and family prayed, lifting me up to the Lord. There were good people looking after me. When you live in a small town, everyone knows everyone. They cared. It made a difference.

When I was in the hospital, my mom brought me a book about someone who had been through a lot and survived. The book meant a lot to me, it gave me hope.

Combining all those things, I knew my life and surviving the crash was a miracle. There is no way, except for God protecting me, that I lived. I knew there might be a good reason, but I still had a lot of questions. As a kid, we never went to church much as a family. But I always attended when I visited my Grandma Stierwalt. When I wiggled in the church pew, asking for her Blackjack gum, I was hearing about the Lord and how He loved me. All those years later, after a semi-truck hit my Dodge pickup and nearly took my life, I understood God's grace of sending Jesus to die on the cross for me. I believed in Jesus as my Savior. I believed that He rose again to give me life. I remembered how my Grandma Stierwalt loved Jesus, always praying throughout her day and doing devotions. I knew I loved Him and could trust Him, too. I started going to church with my girls, and we all were baptized. That day, when I was baptized, I felt a big relief. Even my mom, who didn't bring us to church much when I was growing up, now attends more regularly, too. Now, she's a godly woman who goes to church all the time

14. HELPING EACH OTHER

The good Lord has helped me take care of my girls. My kids have been such a blessing. If it weren't for them, I don't know where I'd be.

Not one to ask for help, I have taken care of them by myself all these years. It's just been us. I have rarely gone out on dates in all this time. I have custody of them, and we live on 160 acres of land I bought with the settlement money. I ended up divorcing my wife, who still uses drugs and is entangled in that lifestyle. When we split up, Delaney was about six, and Hadleigh was about three. Hadleigh doesn't remember much of her mom, but Delaney does. They don't see their mom and wish she would get better. I wish she'd get better, too. I've had to let go and forgive her for the ways she's living, or I would be miserable.

Life as a single dad is not easy, but we all help each other out. I had to do the school thing, dropping off the girls and picking them up. Fortunately, as a maintenance scheduler at Armstrong Flooring, I could set my own schedule, which allowed me to be there for the girls. I don't live like a millionaire, my house is not luxurious. Not living an extravagant life, we live simply in our 1000-square-foot home with a metal roof, one day at a time. I love where I live. The acreage is half-wooded with deer on it and has a pond. I have six cows and used to have horses. For about a year, the girls liked horses but then got tired of them. When we first moved in, neither bedroom had a closet. I hired someone to build them. When the girls were pretty young, they learned to help around the house. They did laundry long before other kids their age and put up dishes. These girls woke themselves up, got dressed, and caught the bus by 7 am.

"I will help you if you help me," I said. "I will work hard and take you to events if you will help with the house and do laundry."

At first, living out in the country was hard, and the girls complained.

"Living here sucks. I don't want to live here. All my friends live in town." Over time, they got used to country life, we have lived here for ten years.

My girls may not have had the best of everything growing up. I am a guy, not always knowing. I did my best, though. If we would go clothes shopping for school, I have to ask them, "Will you wear this?" If they said yes, then I would put the item into the cart.

The one thing that I always sucked at was doing their hair. My kids had a ponytail. Sometimes I braided their hair, but that was about the best I could do. I just couldn't figure it out. Delaney, her hair was so sensitive. She'd be crying when I tried to fix it. Hadleigh, her hair was tough. It took a lot to take out the knots. If they had school pictures, I would take them to their aunt, who fixed their hair. As they grew older, they styled it themselves.

I taught them not to whine and to do their best, and they've taken that advice to heart.

"Nobody likes whiners," I told them. It's cool that something I taught them, they've taken it and made it their own.

When Hadleigh was six or seven years old, I enrolled her in John Casablanca School of Arts in Tulsa. They taught her to hold her head high and not let people talk down to her. She got invited to a pageant in Oklahoma City. What I thought was practice on a Saturday for the Sunday event turned out to be the real thing. My girls were crying.

"Dad, you should have paid attention!"

She didn't have a dress or anything. I had two hours to find her one. The dress shops were closed. In a mall, we searched four places, finally finding a dress. It wasn't the fanciest dress, but it was still a dress for twenty dollars. In two hours, we got the dress and shoes and found some jewelry. It was costume jewelry, but it worked.

Desperate, I called my sister-in-law. "Can you come and do her hair?

"I'm on my way." She came, helping us out.

Getting her dress on and fixing her hair took time, right up to her scheduled spot. The judges were waiting for her to get on stage.

When the judges asked her a few questions, she confidently nailed it. She won the pageant! Because she won, she earned a trip to Orlando, Florida. We visited Disney and got to see the princesses. During the competition, organizers kept those girls on a tight schedule. Hadleigh could have been in ten events, which included things like hospitality, courtesy, and picture taking, but she chose to enter only three of them.

Hadleigh didn't do as well in the competition and didn't want to continue. I found out later that those parents who paid for all ten events, their girls won the whole shebang. I hope she still had a great experience learning how to hold her head high.

As teenagers now, my girls are hard workers, still helping out at home and doing well in school and sports. Hadleigh is enthused about softball and plays basketball. I'm proud of her that she's hitting the weight room. She's getting built, determined like I was when I was a kid. She's getting straight A's in high school.

At 19, Delaney is still figuring out what to do, she is attending school to be an esthetician. She still helps me watch out for myself.

If I am doing something dumb, she'll say, "Really, Dad? Really?"

They both help me watch my spending. I don't need a lot. When I'm by myself, I don't spend much. I had to break down and buy myself a new pair of jeans. The old ones had holes in them. I wear shirts I've worn for ten years. I've always provided well for my daughters, though. Their closets are full. One day one of them asked me to throw away the empty shoe boxes. She had fifteen pairs of shoes!

I worked for Armstrong Flooring for sixteen years, showing up and doing my job. Sometimes, when someone on the maintenance staff wasn't doing their job, I did it for them. One day it was snowing, and I asked the maintenance guy if he could change the valve because it wasn't operating correctly.

He said, "I'm not feeling well."

I did it myself. Taking one wire down at a time, I removed the valve and fixed it. The maintenance guy turned me in. Because I was not an authorized electrician, the boss fired me. God has my timeline written out. That was a step in my life to something different. Two years later, that plant closed down. When I left that job, I had four weeks' vacation.

With the money from the lawsuit settlement, we've been able to take a few vacations to the beaches in Galveston and Alabama and other places. We went to a big amusement park in Ohio and on a cruise to Alaska. My oldest daughter Brittnee came with us a few times. I like the beach, but got tired of going there. It's summer, and where do I go, somewhere where it's hot?

When we traveled to Alaska, I told my daughters, "I don't care where we go, I just want to go fishing one day."

Mostly winging it and not scheduling everything out, we went to a salmon bake, where the girls panned for gold, and watched whales in the ocean. That was awesome, seeing them whales jumping out the water, with water spouting. Fishing was cool. We got wore out, reeling in the halibut. We each caught our limit that day. And even though the girls were getting tired, they stuck with it. On another day, we shopped in Canada. I was amazed at how clean they keep the streets. There was no trash on the ground, and all the grass was cut nicely. It was an awesome trip.

I don't know how I worked sixteen years inside at Armstrong Flooring. When I was a kid, I always liked being outdoors, playing in the creek with my cousins, and hunting.

When Armstrong ended, I worked on the roustabout in the oil fields, which entailed moving heavy equipment and backhoeing. It was backbreaking. Doing a lot of overtime, I missed my girl's games and activities. When I was laid off with them, I started a job on a ranch in 2021, caring for cattle and hauling hay. The funny thing is the owners are my ex-wife's parents. I get along with them fine.

15. THRIVING ON THE RANCH

I love nature so much, and I love my work on the ranch. I don't like the 100-degree heat in the summer. Sometimes it's miserable, especially if it's hot and humid or when the air conditioner breaks in the tractor. I don't get paid as much as I did working in the oil fields, but I am happy. It's worth so much more being happy than making big money. I like being outside. Working at Armstrong, you could get lazy, waiting for something to break on the machines. But now, hauling hay and tending the cattle, I know I've worked hard, and I sleep well at night. If I asked for help, I probably could get home sooner. I'm too hardheaded, though. I still do everything myself, just like I did growing up, feeding the horses and the greyhounds as a kid in Foraker, Oklahoma, and hauling hay for my uncle Mark. He taught me to show up and labor together to get the job done. As I've gotten older, I stopped caring about what people think of me, no longer the "Most Shy" I was in high school. People may start rumors, but I don't pay them mind. My life is between me and the big man upstairs. I do my thing, always putting in 110 percent, like my football coach, Matt Holland, expected us to do in practice. I'm glad God put him in my life. I'm a firm believer that whoever is brought into our lives is there for a reason.

I believe Gary, my boss on the ranch, is in my life for a purpose as well. He is my ex-wife's father. When I was married, I was closer to him than I was to my dad. He has three daughters and no sons. He expects a lot from me, to know which calf goes with which mama in a whole group of cows. And how to fix things on the property. I need to make a list to keep track of everything. I'm a firm believer in writing stuff down. As he's getting older, he's in his seventies now, he is giving me more responsibility. He's even asked if I will take care of the ranch, which has been in his family for three or four generations when he passes on. I'm confident that I can do the work, I just need more time to learn everything.

His wife Ivy is such a good cook, always making breakfast sandwiches in the mornings and other meals. Always the ranch cook, she gets up at five o'clock to feed the crew. Every time we eat at the house, she goes overboard, with enough to feed twenty more people than what is at the table. She's been good to my girls, too, supporting them and helping them get places. She buys clothes for them. My girls love their nana, she's about the best mother figure they've had.

When I talk about surviving that crash, it brings me to tears. I want to tell my story so somebody might believe and get saved. My head, where I had a quarter-size hole from the accident, rarely hurts anymore, and there are few complications. Most of my memories came back. If I do have memory issues, it's because of my older age. I'm 48 now. My ankle, though, still swells up to twice the size of the other ankle, making it difficult to wear boots. Sometimes it will be so tight inside that I roll my foot. It won't ever be the same. If I climb too many stairs or walk too much, I suffer for two to three days. I still can't run. But the pain doesn't stop me.

I still get up every morning, ready to haul hay in the hot sun. I work six days a week, taking Sundays off to go to church and to rest and rejuvenate. When I'm not laboring in the hot sun, I'm at home with my girls. I go through daily Bible verses and watch these YouTube videos, like Phil Robertson, that Duck Dynasty dude. I like listening to him preach. I'm not praying for material things, but I always pray for my family and friends and my boss. Some people think they will get into heaven with good works. That's not what the Bible says. The Bible says: "Believe in the Lord Jesus, and you will be saved."

My family, all of them, are serving the Lord now. Maybe my accident spurred them to get closer to God. My mom and Dad are going to church, something I didn't see much growing up. Mom, she's worked as a secretary for the oil fields for thirty or forty years and is getting ready to retire soon. Dad's making good money in management selling chemicals for oil refineries. My brother Shane is a big rancher. Sometimes, he's got too many irons in the fire. He's got a bunch of kids. He came to know the Lord and got baptized a few years ago. We share a lot of spiritual conversations. And my baby sister Amanda Jo, who is married with a couple of kids, she's always telling me how good I was to her.

I want this book to touch Brittnee, my oldest daughter. I want her to know that I still love her and want the relationship back that we used to have.

My younger girls are getting older now and often are busy with their lives. I have only a few more years with them. We still live under the same roof, abiding by the same rules and helping each other. When I worked in the oil fields, doing a lot of overtime, I missed a lot of my daughter's events. I have asked Gary at the ranch for time off so I can attend their games and events, just like my parents supported me at my ball games in high school. When my daughters leave, I know I'll feel lonely. It's just been us for all these years. I don't need a lot. I would like to find someone to grow old with. That will happen when the good Lord decides it's time. If I ever meet another woman like my Grandma Stierwalt, I will marry her in a heartbeat. She was a good woman, always praying, reading her Bible, and talking to Jesus. She's my model for my life.

She left a legacy in the way she lived. I wholeheartedly agree with what my sister Amanda Jo said at her funeral all those years ago.

"Lois Stierwalt, many words could define her. Loving. Kind. Smart. Devoted. The best values, morals, and principles. Faithful. And the one that sticks out in my mind is her integrity. She helped to define all of those words in our lives. She built the foundation of our family on loving God, diligently studying His word, and then living by it. She had several daily devotionals and found herself in prayer multiple times a day.... She truly set an example by being the best wife, mother, daughter, grandma, friend, anything she needed to be. I know as we mourn her, she would want us to be happy with her new life. While there will never be another soul so precious, I hope that we can touch the lives of others, as she helped change all of our community for the better. The best piece of advice she always emphasized to me is to love God, love your family, and value the blessings in your home. Always tell your momma and daddy "thank you" for all they do for you. Never crowd God out of your life. Allow Him to be the centerpiece. I feel the greatest thing we can do to honor her life is to try and be the best Christians we can, allowing her legacy to live through us."

My Grandma Stierwalt prayed for me when I was a kid, growing up in Foraker, Oklahoma, with my mom and Dad, brother and sister. She took me to the Nazarene church she had attended for fifty years so I could hear about the Lord. And I believe when the semi-truck smashed my truck and nearly took my life, that her prayers and the good Lord spared me so I could get to know Him as my Lord and Savior and carry on her legacy.